D1319081

HA!! HA!!

TICKLES

Funnies

Laugh!!

Tee-Hees

Giggles

For Alexander Cook
– K. H.

For Molly, Maggie, and Joseph Stromoski
– R. S.

Text copyright © 1998 by Katy Hall
Illustrations copyright © 1998 by Rick Stromoski

First edition 1998

Library of Congress Cataloging-in-Publication Data

Hall, Katy.
Really, really bad sports jokes / Katy Hall ; illustrated by Rick Stromoski. — 1st ed.
p.   cm.
Summary: Vampires race neck and neck, Dr. Jekyll plays Hyde and seek,
and cheerleaders drink root beer in this collection of sports gags.
ISBN 0-7636-0433-X
1. Riddles, Juvenile. 2. Sports — Juvenile humor. [1. Sports — Wit and humor.
2. Jokes. 3. Riddles.] I. Stromoski, Rick, ill. II. Title.
PN6371.5.H34867   1998
818'.5402 — dc21   97-23560

2 4 6 8 10 9 7 5 3 1

Printed in Hong Kong

This book was typeset in Soupbone.
The pictures were done in watercolor, pen, and ink.

Candlewick Press
2067 Massachusetts Avenue
Cambridge, Massachusetts 02140

REALLY, REALLY BAD SPORTS JOKES

Katy Hall

illustrated by Rick Stromoski

CANDLEWICK PRESS
CAMBRIDGE, MASSACHUSETTS

CONTENTS

Ready, Set, Laugh!

Why do joggers like fast food?
Race over to pages 8–9
and find out!

What kind of umpires live
at the North Pole?
You'll find this and other hits
on pages 10–11.

Going Batty

Tennis Tee-Hees

How does a tennis player sneeze?
We serve up the answer on
pages 12–13.

What do cheerleaders eat
for breakfast?
You'll cheer when you
find out on pages 14–15.

HA! HA! RAH! RAH!

The Dream Team

Where does the mummy swim team swim?
You'll see when you read the
monstrous riddles on pages 16–17.

What do you call the
toughest football team in town?
You'll get a kick out of the
answer on pages 18–19.

Touchdown Tickles

What's a toad's favorite sport?
Don't croak when you read
pages 20–21.

What kind of bell never rings?
Exercise your fingers by
turning to pages 22–23.

Which basketball player wears
the biggest sneakers?
You'll make an extra point for
laughing on pages 24–25.

What's a baby's favorite stroke?
You can get in the swim on
pages 26–27.

What's the hardest thing about
learning to ride a horse?
Trot over to pages 28–29 and see.

What's invisible and plays
ice hockey?
Turn to pages 30–31
before you freeze!

8

Why do joggers like fast food?
Because they like to eat and run!
Where do trains race?
At a track meet.
What school subject do runners like best?
Jography.
Why did the jogger go to the veterinarian?
Her calves hurt.
What's the best way to win a race?
Run faster than everybody else.
How do tiny little bugs start a race?
One, two, flea . . . go!

11

13

15

TOUCHDOWN TICKLES

What do you call a 250-pound football player with a nasty temper?

"Sir."

What do you call a 250-pound football player whose helmet is on too tight?

Call him anything you want—he can't hear you!

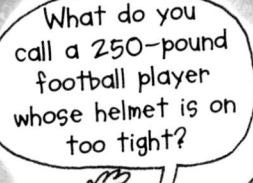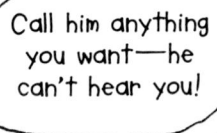

Why is an airline pilot like a football player?

They both want to make safe touchdowns.

What do you call th toughest football team in town?

The All-Scars!

Why don't skeletons play football?

They can't make body contact.

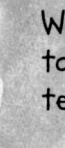

What has [twe]nty-two legs and goes, "[c]runch, crunch, crunch"?

A football team eating potato chips.

How can you tell if there's a football team in your bathtub?

You can't close the shower curtain!

Why is a broken gumball machine like a football player?

Because you always get a quarter back.

How many feet are there in a football field?

It depends on how many people are standing in it.

Do you sell football shoes?

Of course! What size does your football wear?

What position do you play on the football team?

Uh . . . sort of crouched down and bent over.

What football team do ants root for?
The Giants.

FOOLISH FAVORITES

What is Dr. Jekyll's favorite sport?

Hyde-and-seek

What sport do horses like best?

Stable tennis.

What's a pumpkin's favorite sport?

Squash

What's a toad's favorite sport?

Croakquet!

What's a hog's favorite sport?

Pig-Pong.

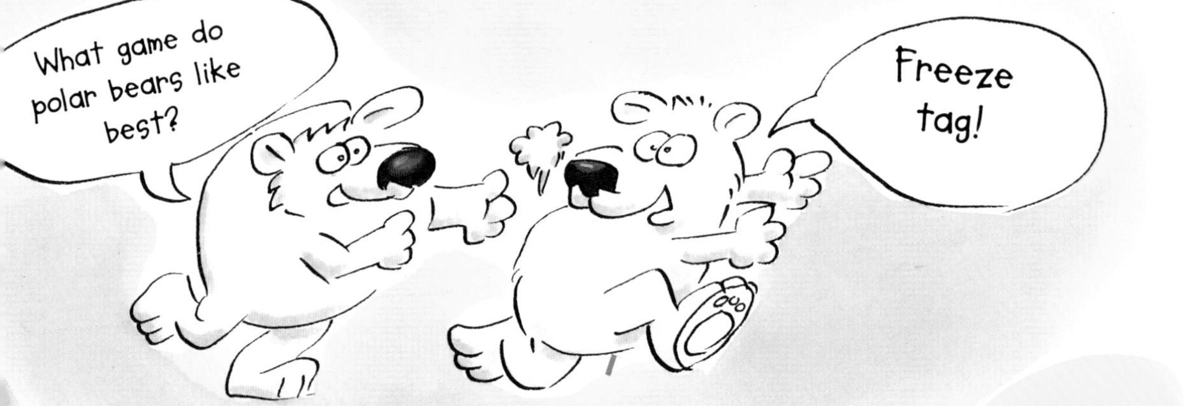

What's a prize fighter's favorite dog?

A boxer.

What's a sumo wrestler's favorite dog?

A husky.

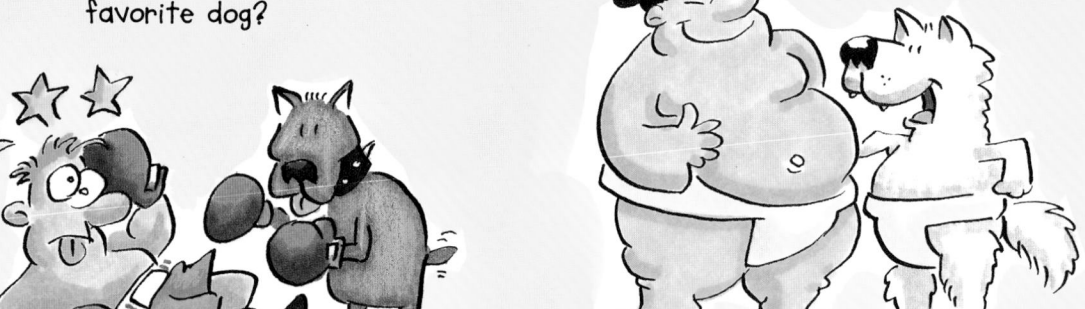

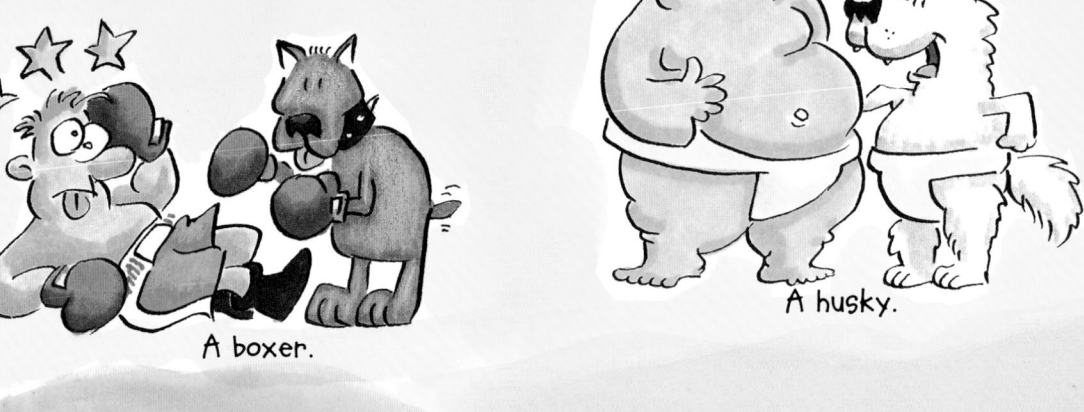

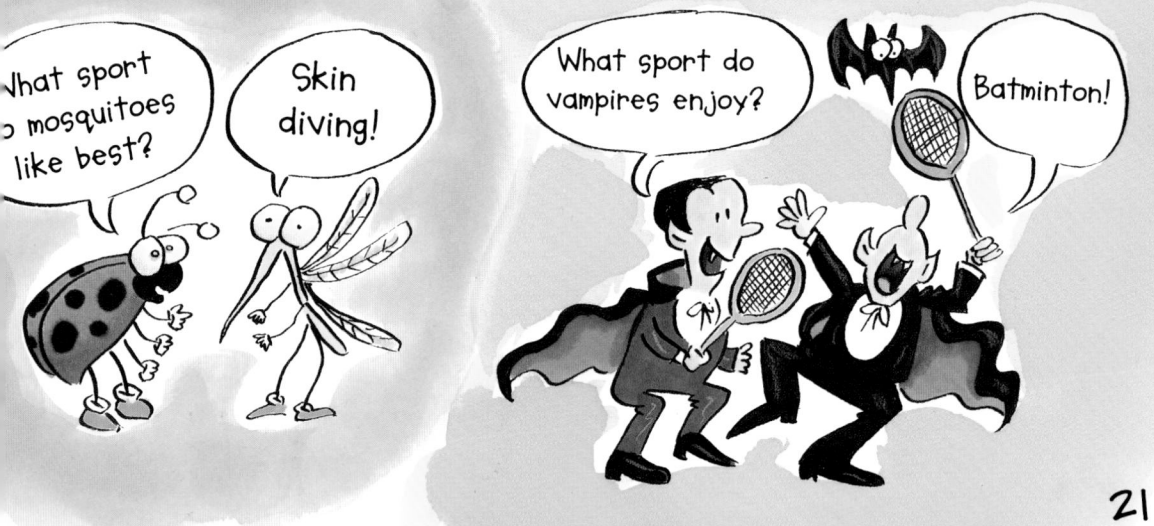

23

27

Galloping Giggles

What sickness can you get from riding wild horses?

Broncitis.

Why are horses so poorly dressed?

Because they wear shoes without socks.

What horse can you ride by moonlight?

A night mare.

Why was the little horse sad?

Because whenever it wanted something, it's mother said **"Neigh!"**

What did one trotter say to the other?

"I forget yo name, but yo pace is famili

Why are lollipops like racehorses?

Because the more you lick them, the faster they go.

Why didn't the filly say much at dinner?

Because she was just a little horse.

Why did the rider ride his horse?

Because the horse was too heavy to carry.

What horse has six legs?

Every horse! Forelegs in front and two legs in back.

What kind of horse comes from Pennsylvania?

A Philly.

What's the hardest thing about learning to ride a horse?

The ground.

30